The Heart's Compass
For the Child Lightworker

Written by Donna Sven

Copyright© 2024
All rights reserved. No part of this book may be reproduced or used in any manner without the prior written permission of the copyright owner, except for the use of brief quotations in a book review. Mystic Me LLC

ISBN: 979-8-9915853-5-4

A note from the Author

"When we are young, we often connect with our spirit in natural and effortless ways. I remember experiencing sparks of psychic downloads as a child, with few references to understand them. As I grew, I noticed that when I was still, I would receive information that always came true. Learning to lean into these feelings helped me strengthen and receive even more downloads. It's like a psychic muscle; by understanding it, you can develop and grow it further. This trust added confidence and a sense of direction to my life. Many synchronicities began to appear, guiding me forward like breadcrumbs, reassuring me that I was on the right path. It's a magical world out there if you're willing to tap in, believe, and trust in yourself.

This book is written to help inspire you to grow with your gifts, rather than apart from them. It explains the how, the what, and the why behind nurturing your unique abilities. Much love on your path forward!

Author & Intuitive,
Donna Sven

Dedication

To the parents who are guided to empower their children with the knowledge to grow their gifts internally, without barriers—may your journey be filled with love, and may you continue to foster a world of peace and understanding.

Table of Contents

1- Introduction --- 1

2- We Are Energy -- 3

3- When We Lose Someone ----------------------------- 9

4- The Power Of Positive Vibes ------------------------ 15

5- The Ways We Naturally Connect -------------------- 21

6- We Have Help --- 35

7- The Bonds We Have On Earth ---------------------- 43

8- Types Of Intuitive Powers And
    How To Strengthen Them ---------------------------- 49

9- Tapping In And Connecting ------------------------- 57

10- The Importance Of Connecting To Others -------- 69

11- Find your magic -------------------------------------- 77

This book is designed to be a companion on your journey of growth and discovery. You may not grasp everything at first, and that's perfectly okay. The beauty of this book is in its ability to evolve with you. As you grow older and your understanding deepens, you can return to its wisdom and insights, finding new meanings and guidance that resonate with your expanding gifts and experiences. You can revisit it time and time again, with each visit unveiling new layers of understanding and inspiration.

Introduction

Did you ever just get a message in your head that came out of nowhere? Like a download, that fills you with knowledge and insight without you even needing to ask. It's as if the universe is whispering in your ear, "Here's something important for you to know."
This is your intuition. Sometimes called psychic abilities or god spark. Many people believe that children are less busy and set in their ways, they play more, around nature more making it easier for them to connect to their abilities. If you know you have these gifts, or can relate to some of the information in this book, then, you can learn to grow them. The more you tap into these gifts and trust what you are given the stronger your gift will become.

WE ARE ENERGY

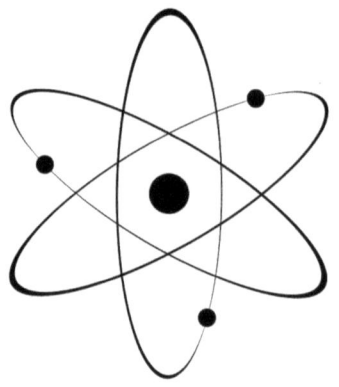

Energy

We are all made of energy. Energy can change forms but can never be created or destroyed—this has been scientifically proven. Even though we have physical bodies that we can see and touch, we are so much more than that. Our true essence, our light, and energy go beyond just our bodies. Our spirit energy allows us to feel emotions, think creative thoughts, and connect with others on a deeper level. It's like an invisible force that flows through us and around us, linking us to the world and each other. This energy makes us unique and special, giving us the ability to love, dream, and be happy.

Energy and light

Each of us has a shining light inside that radiates outward like a beautiful, colorful lantern. This light is our energy, and it surrounds us, making us feel alive and connected to everything around us. When we smile, laugh, or show kindness, our light shines even brighter, and we can feel its warmth and positivity.

Your "spirit light" is part of your intuition and consciousness. It's who you truly are inside and beyond this world. Your intuition is like a magical compass that guides you with feelings and helps you understand the world. As we grow older, many people move away from what they feel and rely more on what they are taught. But you don't have to do that—you can stay connected to your inner light and trust your intuition.

Aura

This invisible light that extends outside a person's body is called "aura." The aura is your inner light shining through. Every person has an aura from their spirit which surrounds their body because it's part of our energy. Your aura is like a colorful bubble that changes with your feelings and thoughts. When you're happy and excited, your aura might shine brightly with happy colors. When you're sad or tired, your aura might be a little dimmer. Some people can see auras and even their colors. Most people feel them. With practice, you can learn to see and feel others' auras more efficiently.

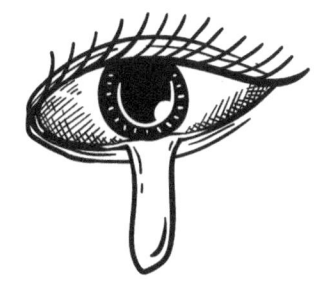

WHEN WE LOSE SOMEONE

Spirit

So, just like the stars twinkle and shine in the night sky, we all have our own light source and energy that makes us special and unique. When someone we love dies or crosses over to the other side, their energy remains intact. Their spirit along with their consciousness does not leave, the energy you felt from them in life continues to exist. If you're very sensitive or through practice you will feel when they are near. It is believed that your aura and the nervous system are interconnected. This is why most people 'feel' energy. When you miss them and think of them you are also sending them a message through your energy. If you pray or just talk to them, they will get your message. Many times, if you ask, you will receive signs from loved ones who have passed. Your love ones can send you many messages, in many different ways. Be open to believing in what you feel.

Understanding Grief and Connecting to Spirit

Grieving is a Part of Life
Sometimes, when we lose someone or something special to us, we feel really sad. This feeling is called grief, and it's something we all go through at some point. It's important to know that it's okay to feel sad and to take time to heal.

Grief and Energy
When we grieve, our energy, or vibration, is lower. This can make it hard to feel connected to the world around us and to the special spirits or loved ones who have passed on. Spirits have to lower their vibration to connect with us, and we have to raise ours. When we are grieving, it's like our vibration is too low for them to reach us.

It's Not That They Aren't There
It's important to remember that our loved ones are not gone and are still trying to connect with us. They are still around us, watching over us, but our sadness sometimes makes it hard for us to feel their presence.

Healing and Reconnecting
As we start to heal and our sadness lessens, our vibration naturally begins to rise again. This makes it easier to feel the love and connection from those special spirits. It's like when the clouds part, and we can see the sun shining through again.

Patience and Love
Be patient with yourself during this time. Allow yourself to feel all your feelings and know that it's a natural part of life. Eventually, you'll feel your light shine bright again, and you'll be able to sense the loving presence of your love one.

When you're feeling sad

When you're feeling sad, upset or disappointed

When you're feeling sad, it can be hard to find inner peace. Remember that it's okay to feel sad sometimes. Find a quiet place where you can sit and take deep breaths, letting the calmness fill your heart. You might feel different, and you might not understand the world you're living in. But remember, many adults feel the same way and don't have all the answers either. It's okay not to know everything. Trust that you are on a journey of learning and growing, just like everyone else. Embrace the love and support around you, and know that it's okay to ask for help when you need it. Life is always changing and moving with energy. Just like the seasons, our lives go through cycles of growth and transformation. Sometimes, things can feel really hard or confusing. But remember, everything that happens is part of a bigger picture. Energy is like a river that flows through our lives, carrying us to new places and experiences. Even when the current is strong and the water is rough, we are being guided to where we need to be. With time, we often gain a better understanding of why certain things happened. What seemed difficult one day might reveal its purpose and lesson later on. Trust in the journey and know that each challenge helps us grow stronger and wiser.

THE POWER OF POSITIVE VIBES

It's best to keep your vibration high. Not weighting yourself down with negativity is very important.

Like we previously said, everything around us, including our thoughts and feelings, is made of energy. This energy has a vibration, which is like a special kind of wave that moves through the air and even through our bodies. Keeping our vibration high is very important because it helps us feel happy and healthy.

Imagine your feelings as different types of music. Happy, positive thoughts are like your favorite upbeat song that makes you want to dance. Sad or angry thoughts are like a slow, gloomy tune that makes you feel down.

When we think positive thoughts and stay happy, we keep our vibration high. This makes us feel good inside and helps us attract other happy and positive people and experiences. It's like being a magnet for good vibes!

But when we let negative thoughts and feelings weigh us down, it's like tuning into that slow, gloomy music. This can make us feel sad or tired and might attract other people and situations that aren't so great.

Remember, your energy and vibration are powerful. Keeping them high will help you feel great and attract positive people and experiences into your life.

Things That Will Raise Your Vibration

Feeling Happy: Think about things that make you happy, Positive Thoughts and Emotions

Healthy Relationships: Kind Friends: Spend time with friends who are kind and make you feel good.

Family Time: Enjoy moments with your family, Spend quality time with your family, whether it's a movie night, game night, or simply having a meal

Good Sleep: Make sure to get enough sleep every night to feel rested and energized.

Taking Breaks: Take short breaks when you're doing something for a long time to relax and recharge.

Eating Healthy Foods: Eating fresh fruits, vegetables, and whole foods can improve your energy levels and overall vibration.

Clean Room: Keep your room tidy and organized so you feel calm and happy. It is important to have a positive Environment.

Positive Media: Watch shows and read books that make you feel good and inspired.

Being Yourself: Do things you love and be proud of who you are.

Playing Outside: Spend time outside, exploring nature, playing in the park, or just taking a walk.

Connecting with Pets: Spend time with your pets. Playing and cuddling with them can bring a lot of joy and comfort.

Be in nature: Enjoy the fresh air and beautiful scenery. Take a stroll along the beach, feeling the sand under your feet and listening to the waves. Observe the plants, flowers, and wildlife around you.

Music: Listening to Uplifting Songs: Play your favorite songs that make you feel happy and energized.

Playing an Instrument: Spend time playing an instrument you enjoy, like the guitar, piano, or drums.

Singing: Sing along to your favorite tunes. Singing can be a great way to release tension and boost your mood.

Freestyle Dancing: Put on some music and dance freely around your room.

Dance Classes: Join a dance class to learn new moves and have fun with others.

Helping Others: Acts of kindness and helping others can greatly uplift your spirit. Whether it's volunteering, helping a friend, or simply sharing a smile, giving to others can enhance your own sense of well-being.

Laughter and Joy: Engage in activities that make you laugh and bring you joy. Whether it's watching a funny movie, playing games, or spending time with loved ones, laughter is a powerful way to elevate your energy.

Creative Expression: Art and other forms of creative expression like writing, crafting, or even cooking. Creativity can be a wonderful way to connect with your inner self and raise your vibration.

Things that Lowers Your Vibration

Negative Thoughts and Emotions
Fear, worry and Sadness: Feeling worried, being sad can make you feel tired, run down and unconnected.

Anger and Frustration: Being angry or frustrated can take away your good energy.
Unhealthy Relationships

Toxic People: Being around people who are mean or make you feel bad can lower your good vibes.

No Boundaries: Not telling others when you need space or time can make you feel overwhelmed.
Stress and Overwork

Burnout: Doing too much without breaks can make you feel really tired and stressed.

Lack of Sleep: Not getting enough sleep can make you feel grumpy and low on energy.

Poor Diet: Eating too much junk food can make you feel sluggish and tired.

No Exercise: Not moving your body enough can make you feel less energetic.

Clutter: A messy room can make you feel stressed and not very happy.

Negative Media: Watching too much bad news or scary shows can make you feel sad, anxious or worried.

Highest Vibration Is LOVE, Lowest Vibration is HATE and FEAR!

THE WAYS WE NATURALLY CONNECT

We connect when we play

The importance of Play

Think back to when you were very young, feeling so happy in that special place within your spirit, a place that was uniquely yours. It felt exciting and good to go there, play with your favorite toy. You were curious about the world, creating your own connections and finding answers through play. This wonderful space is still within reach, it can still be revisited and connected into. Play and imagination frees the mind. It is a special type of meditation when we play. When we engage in play, it allows our minds to relax and wander freely without the constraints of everyday worries. This freedom is crucial for accessing our intuition, as it opens up a space where creative and intuitive thoughts can flow naturally. It is a frequency where your spirit goes into a flow space and you lose time. Play and imagination help us connect with our inner self, the spiritual part of us that holds deep wisdom and intuition. It is part of our heart space. When things get tough, try to get out of your head and into your heart space. This will help you push through difficult times. Through creative activities, we can explore our thoughts and feelings more deeply, leading to greater self-awareness and intuitive understanding. Another way to explain this is, our creative space raises our frequency to our spirit channel.

World of imagination

imagination:

When you play, magic happens—you get lost in your imagination! Time seems to stand still as you create new worlds and adventures in your mind. Like when you were younger pretending to be a superhero, building a castle out of blocks, or exploring a fantastical forest, your imagination takes over and you forget about everything else.
In these moments, you're fully immersed in the joy and wonder of play. You're not thinking about what time it is or what you need to do next. Instead, you're completely present in the moment, letting your creativity and curiosity guide you. Some people get future visions in this special state because it reaches a higher vibration.

The magic of daydreaming

Daydreaming:

Let's us talk about the magic of daydreaming. Imagine sitting in a classroom, and your mind starts to wander off. Instead of listening to what's happening around you, you begin to daydream, floating away into your own imaginative world. This is a special place where you can dream, explore, and wonder without any limits. When you daydream, you're not just imagining things; you're also tapping into a deeper part of yourself called intuition. Some call this a psychic power. Intuition is like a wise, inner voice that sometimes speaks to you through your imagination. As you let your thoughts roam freely, you might come up with new ideas, understand things better, or even solve problems without realizing it. So, the next time you find yourself daydreaming in a classroom, remember that you're not just drifting away—you're also connecting with your intuition and discovering the magic inside you.

The power of creativity

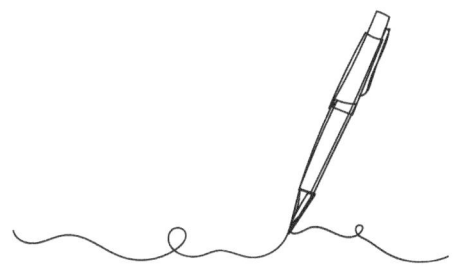

Creative Expression:

Art, music, dance, writing and imaginative play are all ways you can express your inner selves and connect with your spirit. Creativity is like a magical power that lives inside your heart. Imagine a glowing light within you that guides you when you need new ideas or solutions. When you're feeling creative, you're tapping into your spirit light.

This heart space is where your deepest feelings, dreams, and intuition come together. When you connect with it, you can think outside the box and come up with amazing, original thoughts. It's like your inner guide helping you see things differently and find new paths. This is the same space that shares your inner wisdom, your psychic abilities. You could have ideas that just pop into your head during this time, or a buzzing in your ear followed by a message. It will always help you get answers, or creative ideas when you are out of your busy brain and into this space of peace and calm. When your deep into a flow of a project and having joy, It's a meditative state of mind.

Being in nature

NATURE:

Our beautiful Earth is full of life and energy! From the warmth of the sun that makes plants grow, to the wind that makes leaves dance, energy is everywhere. The Earth's energy helps plants, animals, and humans live and thrive. By feeling connected to the Earth, we can tap into its endless supply of positive energy and feel more alive and joyful every day. A short walk can raise your vibration and mood. The exercise can help clear the mind, making it easier to connect with your inner self and enhance psychic awareness. Spending time in nature allows you to connect with the world and feel a sense of wonder and unity with life. Whether it's a walk in the park, a hike in the woods, sitting by the water or simply playing in the garden, nature can be a profound source of spiritual connection. Every living creature has a soul and is made of energy, try to feel each surrounding energy when your alone. Focus on the sounds, smells, and sights around them. Feel their vibrations.

It's Scientific

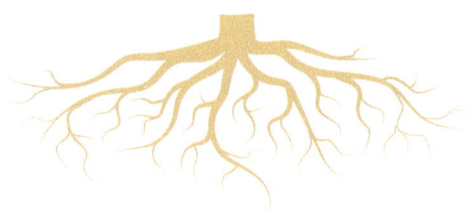

Did you know that trees can talk to each other? It's true! They have a special way of connecting and helping each other out, especially when one of them is sick. Imagine a tree in the forest that isn't feeling well. The trees around it can sense that it's in trouble. So, they send their roots underground to help. These roots connect with the sick tree's roots and share their nutrients. Called the "Wood Wide Web." It's like the internet for trees, where they can send messages and help each other out. By sharing nutrients, the healthy trees can help the sick tree get better.

So, next time you see a forest, remember that the trees are not just standing there—they're looking out for each other, helping their friends stay strong and healthy. It's a beautiful example of how everything is connected.

WE HAVE HELP

OUR ANGELS

Angels:

Angels are beautiful, loving beings who come from a place of pure light. They are here to watch over you and keep you safe. Each person has at least one guardian angel who looks out for them and helps them stay on their true path. Angels can also bring messages of hope, peace, and love, and they are always ready to lend a helping hand whenever you need it. Whenever you feel stuck, sad, or unsure, you can talk to your spirit guides and angels. You might do this through prayer, meditation, or just thinking about them in a quiet moment. They can also send you signs, like a feather on your path, a gentle breeze, or a warm feeling in your heart, to let you know they are there.

Our Spirit Guides

Spirit Guides:

Imagine having a special friend who is always there to help you, even if you can't see them. This friend is called a "spirit guide." Spirit guides are like magical helpers who watch over us and give us guidance throughout our lives.

Spirit guides come in different forms. They can be wise old teachers, loving family members who have passed away, or even friendly animals. Their job is to look out for us, give us advice, and help us make good choices. However, they will not interfere with free will. They might send a gentle nudge or whisper to try and get us into the right direction if we go off path. If we are open and talk to them, they will send comforting thoughts into our hearts.

Even though most can't see our spirit guides, we can feel their presence and know that they are there to support and protect us. It's like having an invisible friend who always has our best interests at heart.

Our Dreams

Vivid dreaming

Dreams are like little movies that play in your mind while you sleep. Sometimes, when we have very clear and colorful dreams, it can feel like a special visit from someone we love who has passed away. These dreams are very clear vivid dreams. When we have a vivid dream that's a visit, we tend to remember it in great detail. When we're awake, we often have our walls up, like a castle with strong walls to protect us. But when we sleep, those walls come down, and we feel safe and peaceful. This makes it easier for us to feel close to our loved ones who have gone to the other side.

our loved ones are using dreams to send us a message, reminding us that they are still with us and watching over us. These magical visits in dreams can make us feel happy, comforted, and loved, even long after we awake.

Try writing down your dreams when you first wake up, before you move around too much. This practice will make remembering your dreams stronger. When you get into a habit of writing your dreams down it creates a memory muscle!

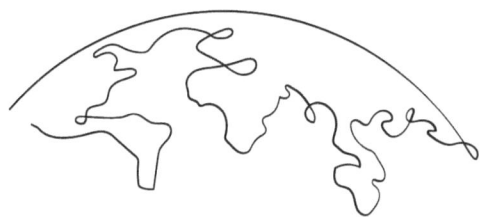

THE BONDS WE HAVE ON EARTH

The soul connection

Soul families

A soul family is a special group of souls who are deeply connected to each other. Imagine having friends and family members who understand you perfectly and support you through everything. These special connections are thought to be planned even before we are born! Choosing to Come Here Before coming to Earth, it is believed that our souls gather together and decide on the roles they will play. This might include being siblings, friends, or even teachers to each other. This plan helps us learn important lessons and grow. When we meet someone from our soul family, we might feel an instant connection, as if we've known them forever. This feeling of connection is a reminder that we are never alone and that we have a special support system in place. It is thought that we come back with the same soul family many times.

Pets and Animals

The Souls of Pets and Animals

Pets as Soul Companions

Just like people, animals have souls too. They are special beings that can bring so much love and joy into our lives. They are very intuitive too! Pets can be a part of our soul family, meaning they share a deep connection with us that goes beyond just this lifetime. This bond is why we feel so close to them and why they can understand us in ways that others might not. They are like little earth guides here to protect us and comfort us when we need them.

Reincarnation of Animals

Some believe that because animals have shorter lives on earth, they can come back more quickly than people after they pass away. It is also thought that, in rare cases, the same animal's spirit can return to our lives within the same lifetime. So, if you ever feel like a new pet reminds you of a pet you had before, it might be because their spirit has returned to be with you again.

Signs of a Reunited Soul

If a new pet acts in ways that remind you of a previous pet, it could be a sign that their spirit has come back. These signs can include similar behaviors, preferences, or even unique habits that only your past pet had.

The Unbreakable Bond

Whether or not our pets come back to us in the same lifetime, the love and bond we share with them never really go away. They remain a part of our soul family forever. Be sure you will see them again!

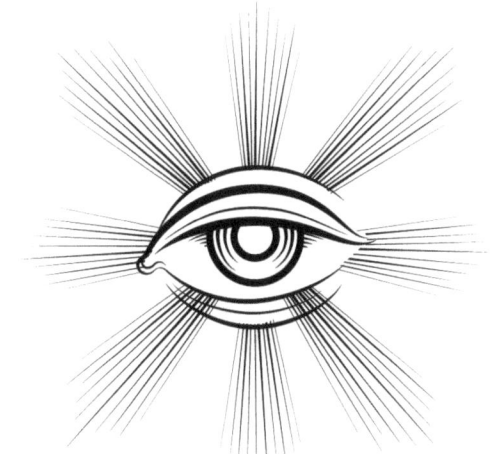

TYPES OF INTUITIVE POWERS AND HOW TO STRENGTHEN THEM

Psychic Abilities

Everyone possesses these gifts, though some may be more recognizable than others. Some people are aware of their gifts but feel afraid, while others don't believe and close the door on learning about them.

Everyone has the right to feel however they want about psychic abilities, including you. If you're willing to practice and believe, you can develop your gifts and become more aware. Psychic abilities are tools you have and can use throughout your life.

The six main intuitive gifts people have are: seeing, Hearing, feeling, knowing, tasting, smelling

Intuitive gifts and their names

Clairvoyance (Clear Seeing)
Meaning: The ability to receive intuitive information through visual images or symbols. People with clairvoyance might see visions, colors, or symbols in their mind's eye.
Example: Seeing a visual image of a loved one's face or an event that is about to happen.

Clairaudience (Clear Hearing)
Meaning: The ability to hear voices, sounds, or music that provide intuitive information. This can be heard internally or externally.
Example: Hearing a voice giving advice or hearing a song that has significant meaning.

Clairsentience (Clear Feeling)
Meaning: The ability to sense feelings or emotions intuitively. This can include physical sensations or emotional impressions.

Example: Feeling a sudden warmth or a chill when entering a room, indicating an energetic presence.

Claircognizance (Clear Knowing)
Meaning: The ability to know something without any logical basis. This is often described as a sudden understanding or insight.
Example: Having a strong gut feeling about a situation or knowing the answer to a question without prior knowledge.

Clairgustance (Clear Tasting)
Meaning: The ability to taste something without actually putting it in your mouth. This can provide intuitive information through taste.
Example: Tasting a flavor that reminds you of a loved one who enjoyed that food, providing a connection to their spirit.

Clairalience (Clear Smelling)
Meaning: The ability to smell scents that are not physically present. This can be a way to receive messages through smell.
Example: Smelling a familiar perfume or flower associated with someone who has passed away

Examples of Clairvoyance (Clear Seeing)

-Imagine you're playing in your room when suddenly, you get a strong feeling that your aunt, who lives far away, is about to visit. You rush to tell your parents, "I think Aunt Emma is coming to visit us today!"

Your parents laugh and say, "That's unlikely. Aunt Emma lives so far away." But a few hours later, there's a knock on the door, and it's Aunt Emma, standing there with a big smile. Your parents are amazed and ask, "How did you know Aunt Emma was coming?"

You shrug and say, "I just had a special feeling inside me."

This ability to sense a surprise visit without any prior information is another example of clairvoyance. It's like having a special sense that helps you know things before they happen.

-Imagine your beloved dog, Max, went missing one afternoon. You searched everywhere but couldn't find him. Suddenly, you get a strong feeling or a vivid image in your mind that shows you exactly where Max is. You tell your parents, "I think Max is at the park near the big oak tree!" They decide to trust your special feeling and head to the park. When you arrive, there's Max, happily playing near the big oak tree, just like you "saw" in your mind.

Your ability to know where Max was without any clues or information is an example of clairvoyance. It's like having a special sense that helps you find things and loved ones that are hidden from everyone else.

Clairvoyance can be a wonderful gift, helping you see things more clearly and understand the world around you in a special way.

Examples of Clairaudience (Clear Hearing)

1-Imagine you're trying to solve a puzzle, and you're really stuck. Suddenly, you hear a soft voice in your mind giving you a hint, like "Look at the blue piece." You follow the hint and find the blue piece fits perfectly, helping you solve the puzzle! This is an example of Clairaudience, where you "hear" helpful guidance in your mind.

2-Imagine you're sitting quietly in your room, and suddenly you hear a gentle voice in your mind that gives you helpful advice or guidance. For example, you might hear a voice saying, "Don't forget to bring your umbrella today." You follow the advice, and later that day, it starts to rain, just as the voice predicted.

3-You might be about to make a decision when you hear a voice in your mind warning you to be cautious. For example, you might hear, "Wait before crossing the street." You pause and realize a car was about to speed by, avoiding a potentially dangerous situation.

Clairaudience can be a wonderful gift, allowing you to hear things that can guide and support you.

Example of Clairsentience (Clear Feeling)

1-Imagine you're playing with your friends, and suddenly you get a strong feeling that your best friend is sad, even though they haven't said anything. You go over to them and ask if they're okay, and they tell you they were feeling a bit down. This is an example of Clairsentience, where you "feel" the emotions of others, even without them telling you.

2-Sensing Energies in a Place: You walk into a room for the first time and immediately feel a sense of warmth and happiness, even though the room is empty. You later find out that the room is where family gatherings and joyful events usually take place, and you picked up on the positive energy left behind.

3-Feeling Physical Sensations: Imagine you're talking to a friend on the phone who is far away, and you suddenly feel a tightness in your chest. Your friend then mentions that they are feeling anxious and experiencing the same sensation. Your ability to feel what they are feeling is an example of clairsentience.

4-Knowing Something is Wrong: You're going about your day when you suddenly get a strong feeling that something is wrong with a loved one. You call them, and they tell you they were in an accident but will be ok . Your feeling alerted you to their distress before you had any logical reason to know.

Clairsentience can be a wonderful gift, helping you understand and support the people around you through your special feelings. Most people have the gift of Clairsentience

Example of Claircognizance (Clear Knowing)

Imagine one day you're sitting in class, and out of nowhere, you just "know" the answer to a question the teacher hasn't even asked yet. You put your hand up and say the answer, and the teacher is amazed because you were right!

Here's how you can tell if you have the gift of claircognizance:

Sudden Knowledge: Sometimes, you suddenly just "know" things without anyone telling you. It might feel like a light bulb turning on in your mind.

Strong Feelings: You get strong feelings or thoughts that something is going to happen, and it does! For example, you might "know" that you'll have a surprise test or that a friend needs your help.

Trust Your Instincts: Whenever you have a strong feeling about something, trust it. Pay attention to how often your instincts are correct. This special feeling is a sign of claircognizance.

Remember, having claircognizance is like having a magical gift that helps you "know" things without being told. It's a special ability that makes you unique and can help you in many ways.

Claircognizance can be a wonderful gift, providing insights, ideas, or information that seem to come out of nowhere.

TAPPING IN AND CONNECTING

Connecting

Catching fireflies

Imagine you're outside on a warm summer night, holding a little jar, waiting to catch fireflies. You know those tiny glowing bugs that light up the night? If you run around too quickly and chase them without paying attention, they often slip away, and you might miss them. But if you sit quietly, stay calm, and just watch, you'll see them light up and come to you. It's that calm feeling in between when your waiting. It's the place where you are present in the moment and open for the next firefly. This place of Being and clearing your mind is the frequency. It's when you let go of all the noise and busy thoughts in your head, you create a calm, peaceful space inside you. In this quiet space, ideas and insights—like the fireflies—start to appear, glowing softly. If you wait patiently, those little sparks of intuitive light will come to you, bringing you understanding and inspiration. So, just like catching fireflies, when you let go, stay still, and simply enjoy the moment, you open yourself up to wait for the next spark of light and wisdom that are all around you.

Just allow

Most people don't usually hear a voice out loud when they receive an intuitive answer. Instead, the answer comes to them in their thoughts. An example would be to sing 'Happy Birthday' in your head. You don't hear the song with your ears, but you can still 'hear' it in your mind. This is how most people hear with their intuitive gifts. Similarly, when you ask a question and wait for an answer, it often appears in your thoughts as a quiet and clear idea. It's like having a conversation with yourself without using your voice. Pay attention to your first thought or word you hear. Usually its the first answer you get without going into thinking about the question. Just allow it, the more you practice the stronger this skills will get.

I just got chills

Have you ever heard someone say, 'I just got chills when you said that'! Pay attention to goosebumps or chills when you feel something strongly. Many times, your guides will signal a 'yes' in this way. When you feel in your gut that something you're saying is correct, you might get chills or goosebumps. This is a conformation from your guides, showing that you're connected to your intuition and are on the right track. If you have a problem or a friend asks for advice, see if they confirm these feelings too.

Guessing games

Play guessing games where you try to predict the outcome of simple situations, like what color a traffic light will be when you approach it or what the weather will be like tomorrow. What parking spot will mom or dad get, try to feel what direction the parking spot will be.

Writing your thoughts

Automatic writing is a way to let your hand move freely to write or draw without thinking about it too much. It's like tapping into your subconscious mind or even connecting with a higher source for inspiration. People use it to get new ideas, messages, or creative thoughts that they might not get through regular writing.

Think of it as opening a special channel that lets your thoughts and feelings flow onto the paper. Some people find it helps them connect with their inner wisdom and creativity. You know you're really tuned in when you write words you don't normally use or even know! Some folks have even written books, movie scripts, and music this way, finding amazing ideas that feel almost magical.

Here are some tips on automatic writing

Imagine that inside you, there's a magical radio that can tune into different special frequencies. Each frequency is like a unique channel filled with different feelings, ideas, and creative energy. Finding your frequency means discovering that special channel where you feel most connected and in tune with yourself. It's where your best ideas and feelings come to life and just flow.
    We are made of energy, and our energy has different vibrations, which means the frequency is on a certain wave. Once you find your frequency, you can practice tuning into it. The more you practice, the easier it will become to tap into the same frequency. Doing a few of the same habits, like writing in your journal, drawing pictures, or meditating before you start can help you connect more easily. It's especially helpful to do these habits in the same room and at the same time each day. For example, after a shower at night when you're alone in your room and it's quiet. This makes it easier to find and tune into your magical frequency and let your creativity flow.
    It's like having a superpower that helps you connect with your inner world and share your special gifts with everyone around you.

Meditation

Meditation and Mindfulness

Meditation is a traditional way to help clear your mind. It's something we sometimes do without thinking, because it involves not thinking! It can be hard at first because we're always busy and have so many thoughts. But if you sit quietly for a few minutes each day, you can get better at it and even start to enjoy it. When you relax and don't focus on anything important, you might find moments of insight and connection.

This could be focusing on your breath, imagining a peaceful place, or thinking about things you're grateful for. To find calm and feel good inside, try some simple steps. First, find a quiet spot where you can sit comfortably. Close your eyes and take a deep breath in through your nose. Hold it for a moment, and then breathe out slowly through your mouth. Keep doing this and feel your body relax.

You can also meditate while listening to soft music or using headphones. The gentle sounds can help you feel peaceful and happy. Try to sit quietly for just 10 minutes each day. It might feel hard at first, but with practice, it will get easier. Through practice your busy brain will stop being so active. Afterward, this time to regroup will help you feel calm and ready for anything!

Synchronicities and Connections

Have you ever noticed when things just seem to fall into place, like magic? That's called synchronicity! It's when events happen at just the right time, and they feel like they are connected in a special way.
For example, you might be thinking about a friend, and then they suddenly call you! Or you might find a book about a topic you've been curious about, right when you needed it. These moments make you feel like everything is connected in a wonderful way.
Connections are like invisible threads that link us to people, places, and even ideas. They help us feel like we belong and that we're part of something bigger. When we pay attention to synchronicities and connections, it can feel like the universe is sending us little messages to guide us.
By noticing these magical moments, you can learn to trust your intuition and believe that everything happens for a reason. It's like having a secret map, saying "you're on track," keep going, and it then leads you to amazing adventures and discoveries!

Examples of Synchronicities

Meeting a New Friend: Imagine you're feeling a bit lonely and wish you had someone to play with. Suddenly, you meet a new friend at the park who likes the same games and toys as you do. It's like the universe knew just what you needed!

Finding a Lost Item: You've been looking for your favorite toy for days, and you can't seem to find it. Then, one day, you decide to clean your room, and there it is, hiding under your bed. It's like the toy appeared right when you were ready to find it.

Hearing a Favorite Song: You wake up with a song stuck in your head, and later that day, you hear the same song playing on the radio or in a store. It's as if the song followed you all day!

Thinking of Someone: You're thinking about a family member you haven't seen in a while, and then you receive a letter or a phone call from them. It's like your thoughts sent a special message to them.

Seeing the Same Numbers: You keep seeing the same numbers, like 11:11 or 3:33, on clocks, license plates, or signs. It's like these numbers are trying to tell you something special.

Finding a Book: You're curious about a topic, and then you visit the library or a bookstore and find a book that has all the answers you were looking for. It's like the book was waiting just for you.

Animals Showing Up: You feel sad or worried, and suddenly, a friendly pet or a cute animal shows up to comfort you. It's like the animals can sense your feelings and want to make you smile.

Helpful Habit

Before bedtime, find a quiet and comfortable place to lie down. Your bed is a perfect spot where you can relax and feel safe.

Close Your Eyes and Breathe

Close your eyes and take a few deep breaths. Inhale slowly through your nose and exhale gently through your mouth. Feel your body relax with each breath.

Imagine a Warm Light

Picture a warm, glowing light surrounding you. This light is filled with love and peace, and it makes you feel safe and calm. Ask that the light to protect you from any negative energy.

Talk to Your Spirit Guides

In your mind, talk to your spirit guides. You can ask them for help, guidance, or simply share your thoughts and feelings. Remember, your spirit guides are always there to listen and support you.

Listen and Feel

After you talk, take a moment to listen quietly. You might not hear words, but you may feel a sense of comfort or get gentle thoughts and ideas. This is how your spirit guides communicate with you.

Say Thank You

When you're done, say thank you to your spirit guides for being there for you. Feel the gratitude in your heart.

THE IMPORTANCE OF CONNECTING TO OTHERS

Even plants connect

Did you know that plants can send messages to each other through the air? When a plant is under attack by insects, it releases special chemicals called volatile organic compounds (VOCs) into the air. These chemicals act like a distress signal, warning nearby plants of the danger.
When other plants detect these chemicals, they can start producing their own defensive chemicals to protect themselves from the insects. It's like plants have their own secret language to help each other stay safe!
Isn't it amazing how nature has its own way of communicating and looking out for one another?

Another example of energy sharing a connection!

Connection with others

We all have invisible strings made of light, connecting our hearts to the hearts of others.
When you're happy and your heart is glowing with joy, your light travels through these strings, reaching others and making them feel happy too. Similarly, when someone else is feeling happy, their light can travel through the strings and make you feel happy as well.
Sometimes, when someone is feeling sad, their energy might travel through the strings and you can feel a bit of their sadness too. This helps us understand and care for each other because we're all connected by these beautiful strings of light and energy.
It's like when you see a friend smile, and you can't help but smile back. That's the magic of our energy, connecting us and helping us share our feelings, even without saying a word.

Sparks of light

Imagine that our words and thoughts are like little sparks of light that travel through the air and touch everything around us. When we think kind thoughts or say nice words, these sparks of light glow brightly and spread happiness and positivity to everyone they touch. But, if we think mean thoughts or say hurtful words, those sparks can turn dark and make others feel sad or upset. It's like sending out tiny storm clouds that can darken someone's day. Our words and thoughts are powerful, just like those sparks, and they can affect the feelings of others.

Sense the good in others

You can sense the good and happy energy in others by being in tune with your own feelings and being open to the energy around you. This is part of your intuition, a special gift that helps you understand and connect with others on a deeper level. When you're in a room with like-minded individuals, your vibration becomes higher and the connection is stronger. Conversely, if you're with others who are sick or not doing well emotionally, you may not realize it, but it's thought that you lower your vibration to match theirs, which can be draining in a heavy environment for a long period of time. It's important to notice this and take breaks to recharge and maintain your own positive energy.

Practicing acts of kindness

Helping others and practicing acts of kindness can truly make a difference in the world. Words matter a lot. If you notice someone is sad, don't join in making them feel worse. Avoid negative conversations about them because words carry energy. Be brave and stand out in the group by showing compassion and empathy. Simple acts, like saying a few kind words, can help someone feel much better and also lift your vibration.

Words and thoughts have power

Just as our kind words and thoughts can make someone happy and brighten their day, our hurtful words and mean thoughts can lower their energy and make them feel sad. This doesn't just impact the person you're speaking to—it can affect everyone around them too. When someone feels sad or hurt, their dark clouds can spread, making the whole group feel less happy.

So, we need to be careful and choose our words and thoughts wisely. By being kind and understanding, we can make sure our sparks of light always spread love and happiness, helping everyone around us feel good. Our words have the power to create joy, but they also have the power to hurt, and this can ripple out and impact others. Let's use our words to make the world a brighter, happier place for everyone!

FIND YOUR MAGIC

Being true to yourself without the pressure of online popularity and ego.

What is Ego? Your ego is like a part of you that always wants to be the best and get attention. It's that voice in your head that sometimes makes you feel like you need to be perfect or better than others. While having confidence is good, too much ego can make it hard to listen to your true self, or intuition.

Connecting with Your Intuition is your inner voice or gut feeling that helps you make good decisions and understand things in a special way. It's like having a superpower that guides you from the inside. To connect with your intuition, you need to be calm and trust yourself.

The internet is a fun place to explore and learn, but it can also make your ego louder and your gifts smaller. Social media, for example, often shows everyone's best moments, which can make you feel like you need to be perfect too. This can distract you from listening to your inner voice. It can pull you away from the true magic in life.

The internet can be used a wonderful tool too.

Share Your Talents: Post your artwork, writing, or music on platforms that encourage creativity. You can inspire others and get feedback on your work. Read about community projects and things that inspire you. Don't follow - lead and be true to yourself.

Your Powerful

Always remember, when we laugh, play, and help others, our light shines bright. Sometimes, when we're feeling tired or a little sad, our light can get a bit dim. But don't worry, because we can always make our light bright again by doing things that make us happy and spending time with people we love. Some people explain this as higher vibration and lower vibration energy, while others call it light and heavy energy. Heavy energy can weigh on you!
There are many ways to lift or lighten your vibration, such as laughing, being around friends and loved ones, spending time with pets, enjoying nature, creating, helping others, exercising, and eating healthy. Do your best to stay away from negative situations and people if you can—anything that makes you feel drained afterward. Remember, you are in control and more powerful than you know.

So, when you're around people, trust your feelings and pay attention to the energy you sense and feel. It's like tapping into a magical world of invisible connections and knowing who makes you feel safe and happy. We are not just our bodies; we are the beautiful, shining light of energy within. This is what gives us our beautiful spirit.

www.ingramcontent.com/pod-product-compliance
Lightning Source LLC
Chambersburg PA
CBHW042332150426
43194CB00001B/26